Nadia Comaneci: Perfect 10

By David Bruce

TABLE OF CONTENTS

Chapter 1: Perfect 10

At the 1976 Olympic Games in Montreal, Canada, Nadia Comaneci (pronounced NAD-ya koh-muh-NECH) was absolutely spectacular as she won five medals. On July 18, competing on the uneven bars, she became the first gymnast ever to score a perfect 10. In fact, the equipment that was set up to display the scores was not programmed to display a score that high. Therefore, the apparatus displayed a score of 1.00, which is a very low score.

Nadia's coach, Bela Karolyi, was shocked by the low score, and he asked for an explanation. A Swedish judge held up 10 fingers to indicate a perfect score. Meanwhile, one of Nadia's teammates told her, "I think it's a 10, but they don't know how to make a 10." Nadia asked Bela, "Sir, is that really a 10?" He replied, "You bet it is, Nadia."

Reflecting on her perfect score 25 years later, Nadia said, "Scoring the 10 was the biggest moment [of the Olympic Games] for me, but at the time I didn't realize how big it was, and how everything was going to change after that."

Everything did change for her. Nadia became an international celebrity, and her photograph appeared on the covers of *Newsweek*, *Sports Illustrated*, and *Time* in the same week. This was the first time that a human being had appeared on the covers of these magazines in the same week. Previously, only a racehorse named Secretariat had achieved that honor. The Associated Press also named her 1976's Female Athlete of the Year.

This is Nadia's story.

Chapter 2: Youth and Early Training

Nadia's parents are Gheorghe and Stefania-Alexandrina Comaneci. He worked as a mechanic on vehicles used in the forest around his hometown, while she worked in an office. Her parents lived in Romania in a small village called Onesti, which is located in the Romanian province of Moldavia and nestled in the foothills of the Carpathian Mountains. In 1952, before Nadia was born, the first President of the Socialist Republic of Romania, Gheorghe Gheorghiu-Dej, decided to build a new industrialized city on the site of Onesti. In 1964, the city's name became officially Gheorghe Gheorghiu-Dej, in his honor, although residents continued to call it Onesti.

On November 12, 1961, Nadia Elena Comaneci was born in Onesti. According to Nadia, "It is a magical place, and I have always felt lucky that I was born there."

Nadia is not a usual Romanian name. When her mother was pregnant with her, she and Nadia's father went to a Russian film that they enjoyed. The name of the heroine of the film was Nadia—which means "hope"—and they decided to name their daughter after her.

Her father was happy with his new daughter although he had hoped for a son. Later, when young Nadia started tumbling rambunctiously around the house like the tomboy she was, her mother told Nadia's father that he already had a son—Nadia.

Even as a two-year-old child, Nadia had the tenacity to get what she wanted. During the holiday season, young Nadia noticed a sweet hanging on the family Christmas tree. She grabbed the sweet, pulled, discovered that it was tied to the tree, and pulled harder, bringing the Christmas tree down on top of her. Her parents quickly rescued her, and they discovered that she had the sweet in her hand—along with part of the branch that it was tied to.

When Nadia was five, Adrian, her brother, was born, giving her father both a tomboy and a real son. When her mother brought Adrian home from the hospital after his birth, he was crying. However, when Nadia held him, he stopped crying. At first, Nadia believed that the stork had brought Adrian to the door of their home, but her parents told her that the stork had brought Adrian by way of the chimney—the soot in the chimney had made Adrian's skin a little darker than Nadia's.

As a young tomboy, Nadia enjoyed climbing trees. Her grandmother once asked her, "Why on earth do you spend all your time climbing trees?" Nadia replied, "Because they're here to be climbed." However, Nadia did grow annoyed when a young boy called up to her, "Hey, Comaneci, want some twigs to build your nest with?" Although Nadia occasionally fell out of a tree, she was never seriously hurt.

Young Nadia could be naughty. At a store, she tried on a pair of roller skates. Because she wanted the roller skates so much, she skated out of the store, forcing her father to pay for them. In addition, one day she stayed outside until after dark, playing, and her parents worried about her. When she finally came home, her father spanked her once, then made her kneel on cracked walnut shells for three hours—so she would be as uncomfortable as he had been waiting for her to return home.

Since the energetic young Nadia had an overabundance of energy—she had broken the springs of four couches in three years by jumping up and down on them—her mother enrolled her in gymnastics. Nadia started studying gymnastics at age three when she was in kindergarten.

(Kindergarten starts early in Romania because mothers work outside the home.)

Nadia's very first gymnastics teacher was Marcel Duncan, a master of motivation. When his young gymnasts did well, he would appear before them at the end of their exercises with his hands behind his back and ask, "Who thinks they did well today?" All the children would raise a hand up in the air, and Mr. Duncan would reveal the bag of chocolates he was hiding behind his back and allow each gymnast to have a chocolate. But if the young gymnasts did not perform well, then there were no hands behind Mr. Duncan's back, and no chocolate.

In 1968, Nadia began training with coaches Bela and Marta Karolyi. Bela discovered Nadia at her school. He traveled from school to school searching for children with the potential to become great gymnasts. At the schools, he would watch the children do tumbling and cartwheels in the playground, and if they showed gymnastics talent, he would take the children's names so he could ask their parents to send them to his gymnastics school. At Nadia's school, he noticed Nadia and one of her friends as they performed gymnastics tricks during recess. Unfortunately, the school bell rang before he could get their names or even see their faces, and the blond-haired children ran back into their school.

Because Bela had been so impressed with the girls, he went from room to room in the school searching for them, but he was unable to recognize them. After two trips through the school looking for the girls, he started asking all the children, "Who likes gymnastics?" The children didn't know what the word "gymnastics" meant, so he started asking them who liked to do cartwheels. Whenever some children said that they liked to do cartwheels, Bela asked them to do a few cartwheels for him. Unfortunately, they weren't the children he had seen during recess.

Finally, he saw a couple of blond-headed children in the back of a classroom. He asked if they knew how to perform cartwheels, they performed a few cartwheels for him, and Bela knew that he had found the girls who had impressed him so strongly. He enrolled them in his gymnastics school, along with 24 other young girls whom he would attempt to train to be world-class gymnasts. Nadia was six years old.

Nadia, of course, became a famous gymnast, but what became of the other little girl? Her name was Viorica Dumitriu, and she became a foremost ballerina of Romania.

Bela did have an entrance exam for his gymnastics school. Girls had to run a sprint of about 50 feet, perform a long jump, and walk on the balance beam. He said, "If they are afraid of the beam, we send them home right away." Nadia wasn't afraid. In fact, after the Montreal Olympics, when Bela was asked if Nadia had ever shown fear, his answer was short and direct: "No."

As Nadia trained with him at his gymnastics school, Bela continued to be impressed with her. He was impressed with her for a very good reason. Whenever he asked her to do something, she never said "No" or "I can't do that." Instead, she tried to do what he asked her to do.

While Nadia was training with Bela, all of her expenses were taken care of by the Romanian government. Nadia's entry fees, coaching, travel, leotards, room and board, and choreography expenses were all paid by the government. Romania was a socialist country, and the government subsidized sports. A stadium and an indoor sports hall were located in every town, and each sports center bore the Latin inscription *Mens sana in corpore sano* ("A sound mind in a sound body").

About a year after Nadia began training with Bela, at her first Romanian National Junior Gymnastics Championships, she placed thirteenth after some falls on balance beam. After she fell off the balance beam, she tried to get back on, but being excited because she was in her first competition, she immediately fell off on the other side. Fortunately, her team still managed to finish in first place.

To ward off the bad luck of Nadia's number 13th finish, Bela gave her an Eskimo doll that he had bought in Holland, saying, "You must never finish thirteenth again." Bela's gift started Nadia's hobby of collecting dolls. By age 14, she owned over 200 dolls, many of them given to her. One doll named Fragolina was so large that it sat on a sofa. By the time Nadia retired from competing in gymnastics, she had collected over 300 dolls.

Bela's training of Nadia quickly paid off. She worked hard, and she finished first in the competition the following year, and she carried the Eskimo doll that Bela had given her to other important competitions. In 1971, after Nadia had finished in first place in the all-around in her age group, she became a member of Romania's national gymnastics team.

During Nadia's early years as a gymnast, the person who pushed her most was her teammate Teodora "Dorina" Ungureanu. Although their rivalry could have made them enemies, they became best friends instead. They competed at many events together, and Teodora was one of her teammates at the 1976 Olympic Games in Montreal, where she won a silver medal on the uneven bars and a bronze on the beam, as well as a team silver. Often, people thought that Nadia worried about competing against such athletes as Nelli Kim, Olga Korbut, and Ludmilla Tourischeva, but she would say, "The only one that can scare me is Teodora." As best friends, they shared similar interests, such as collecting dolls—and trophies and medals.

Nadia and Teodora played the kind of pranks that best friends play. One day, they held their hands together and threw Adrian, Nadia's brother, all the way to the ceiling, where he left a couple of dirty fingerprints. Fortunately, he was not afraid.

The two girls also played soccer against boys, with the losing team buying chocolate bars for the winning team. Because Nadia and Teodora were good soccer players, they usually won the game and enjoyed chocolate bars afterward. After all, Nadia was competitive, and not just in gymnastics. In fact, she had won her very first athletic competition—a tricycle race. When Nadia was young, sometimes the mothers of the boys she played with used to complain that she played too roughly.

In 1972, Nadia competed in her first international competition: the Friendship Cup. She won the gold medal in the all-around, and the Romanian team won the silver medal. This was the start of an international reputation in gymnastics for Romania, a reputation that is still strong today.

Of course, during these years of early training, Nadia was small, but size can be deceptive. At an exhibition in Italy, very few people showed up to watch the Romanian team, because they thought that since they were little girls, they wouldn't be able to do much. Bela was angry when he saw that only 1,500 people had shown up in an auditorium that could seat 10,000. However, the news spread by word of mouth that the Romanian girls could do very impressive gymnastics, and on the second and third days of the exhibition every ticket was sold, leaving standing room only.

In 1974, Americans Rodney and Debbie Hill brought their Denver School of Gymnastics team, the Hill's Angels, to compete in Romania, and they were amazed that the Romanian team appeared to consist of little girls. Rodney even considered asking his wife to not compete because she was an Olympian, and he wanted to make the competition more even; however, the Romanians said that would not be necessary. In the competition, Debbie won only the balance beam—13-year-old Nadia Comaneci won the other three individual apparatus events.

One evening after 10 p.m., when they would normally be in bed, Nadia and Teodora visited Debbie Hill. She was surprised to see them and asked, "How did you get away from home?" They replied, "We snuck out of the dorm." As talented gymnasts undergoing intensive training, Nadia and Teodora lived in a dorm with other gymnasts, instead of at home with their families.

In 1974, Nadia and Teodora also took part in an exhibition in Paris, France. The gymnastics authorities were expecting to see 1972 Olympian Alina Goreac at the exhibition, but instead the Romanians sent Nadia and Teodora. For this trip out of Romania, Nadia's mother baked a batch of her daughter's favorite cookies and packed them for her to take to Paris.

Unfortunately, once Bela and his two gymnasts arrived in Paris, the exhibition turned out not to be well organized. First, no one met them. When a translator finally arrived, Bela, Nadia, and Teodora found out that the gymnastics officials weren't expecting such young gymnasts. Instead, they were expecting an Olympian. Furthermore, the gymnastics officials thought that Nadia and Teodora were just little girls, and so they didn't want them to take part in the major exhibition. Therefore, they sent Bela, Nadia, and Teodora to a minor exhibition.

As asked, Nadia and Teodora performed at the minor exhibition, but then Bela took his gymnasts to the major exhibition. When they arrived there, a guard asked him for a pass. Of course, Bela didn't have a pass because no one had given him one. Therefore, Bela used his prowess as an athlete—he had thrown the hammer in track and field, boxed, and played rugby. He told Nadia and Teodora to stick close to him, and he simply barreled his way into the exhibition hall past the guard.

Once inside the exhibition hall, Bela told Nadia and Teodora to hide behind a pile of mats, then he waited for a chance for them to display their gymnastics skills. A chance occurred after Soviet gymnast Ludmilla Tourischeva performed a vault. After she made her vault, Bela told Nadia to take her place at the starting point of the vault runway—she would vault next.

Nadia performed a perfect Tsukahara vault, astonishing the crowd. Cheers poured from the audience, and the French gymnastics authorities suddenly became very happy to allow Nadia and Teodora to display their gymnastics skills in the main exhibition. A highlight occurred when the two gymnasts performed a floor exercise together. This exhibition provided valuable international experience for Nadia and Teodora.

As a gymnast competing internationally, Nadia often flew. She enjoyed visiting the cockpit when she was allowed, and since she was a celebrity, she was sometimes allowed. She once visited the cockpit of a British Airways Boeing, where she impressed the pilot by questioning him about the complicated instruments he used to fly the plane. A year or two later, the pilot had good reason to remember her visit to his cockpit. He watched her score a perfect 10 during her first day of competition at the Montreal Olympics, and later he said, "I can't tell you how proud I was. My little girl! I could scarcely believe it!"

In 1975, Nadia became eligible to compete at the senior level in international competition. Previously, she had competed at the junior level. In Skien, Norway, she competed at the European Championships, where in an upset victory over Soviet gymnast Ludmilla Tourischeva—who showed good sportsmanship by kissing her on the cheek—she won the gold medal in the all-around. In addition, Nadia won gold medals in balance beam, uneven bars, and vault. She also earned a silver medal in the floor exercise. When the Romanians returned home, crowds of people met them. Members of the Young Pioneers, a group similar to the Girl Scouts, carried a sign that read, *Bravo Nadia! Tot inainte!*" In English, that means, "Bravo, Nadia—once again!"

Obviously, 1975 was a very good year for Nadia, and United Press International named her the Sportswoman of the Year for 1975—she also won in 1976. However, the resulting publicity made Nadia uneasy, and her mother speculated that if there were a tunnel between their home and her school, Nadia would very happily use it to avoid reporters.

In 1976, Nadia entered the American Cup competition at Madison Square Garden in New York City. She earned a perfect 10—the first ever earned in the United States—when she performed a Tsukahara vault. Japanese gymnast Mitsuo Tsukahara, after whom the vault is named, also competed in the American Cup that year. He too performed a Tsukahara vault, but ironically he managed to score only a 9.3. Later, Nadia earned another perfect 10 on the floor exercise, even though three times in a row the wrong music started to play.

For the women, the winner of the American Cup was 14-year-old Nadia. For the men, the winner was 18-year-old American gymnast Bart Conner. In fact, the American Cup competition was held on March 28, Bart's 18th birthday. Standing on the winners podium, Bart and Nadia held their silver cups. A photographer asked Bart to give Nadia a kiss. He did, but Nadia wasn't interested in boys yet. They didn't know it at the time, but later they were to fall in love and be married.

Bart remembers the kiss, but Nadia says she remembers little about it; after all, she was only 14 and still playing with dolls. She said, "I remember it was a blond boy, but there were four blond boys on the American team. They all looked the same to me."

Some of the answers she gave to reporters' questions at the American Cup competition were charming. People tend to have a lot in common no matter what country they are from. When Nadia was asked what was her favorite place in the United States, she replied, "Disneyland." Previously, after the 1972 Olympics, Soviet gymnast Olga Korbut had met United States President Richard Nixon. When reporters asked her about the meeting, she said, "I thought he was nice, but I liked Disneyland better."

Although the Romanians took time out to go to such places as Disneyland, one characteristic of their women's gymnastics team was and is a capacity for hard work. In 1976, the Romanians competed in many small meets as a kind of tune up for the Olympics. One meet was against gymnasts from Great Britain. Once the meet was over—the Romanians won, of course—they didn't leave the gym, but kept on working.

Of course, kids will be kids, even when they are elite athletes. In Romania, Nadia and some other gymnasts did not turn their lights out when they were supposed to—they waited until they heard Bela coming to check up on them, then they turned out the lights. They didn't fool Bela, however, and he told them, "Your light was on. You must not be sleepy. Maybe you need to get a bit more tired before you close your eyes." He made them run for a while outside before he let them go to bed again. The next day the young gymnasts were very tired, and after that they turned out their lights when they were supposed to.

Chapter 3: The Montreal Olympic Games

At the 1976 Olympic Games held at Montreal, Canada, Nadia became an international celebrity. She was well known in the gymnastics world due to her success in international competitions; however, the general public was unaware of her skill in gymnastics. Most members of the general public simply didn't expect the Romanian women to do much in the Olympic Games; after all, they had won their most recent medal back in 1960 and their total Olympic medals consisted of two bronzes.

Before the Olympic Games, reporters asked Nadia how many gold medals she expected to win. Full of confidence, she answered, "Five." Five is the total number of events in which a woman gymnast can win individual gold medals: the all-around, balance beam, floor exercise, uneven bars, and vault. She came close to her goal and won three gold medals, a silver (for the team competition), and a bronze.

Nadia's parents were unable to go to the Montreal Olympic Games with her, as travel was expensive. However, Nadia did write and send a postcard back home to them. In addition, the Olympic Games were televised, so her parents had the opportunity to stay up to watch her. However, only her father watched the Olympics, staying up until 4 a.m. to see her. Nadia's mother didn't want to watch because she was afraid that Nadia would fall. Other Romanians stayed up to watch Nadia, and they telephoned her family very early in the morning to congratulate them on her success. People also sent telegrams to congratulate them. In addition, Nadia's father was recognized by people in the street, who congratulated him.

In 1976, at the Olympic Games, Nadia was only 14 years old. She weighed 86 pounds and stood not quite 5 feet tall. In previous years, gymnasts had been mostly older and bigger. However, in 1972, tiny Olga Korbut electrified the world at the Olympic Games in Munich. This started a trend toward younger, smaller gymnasts who were able to do riskier and more spectacular gymnastics tricks. This trend has lasted to the present day and shows little sign of ending, although the age requirements of athletes permitted to compete in the Olympic Games is going up.

As always, Bela did everything he could to help his team. At workouts before competition, he wanted the audience and media watching the workouts to be on the side of his team. Therefore, he delayed the entrance of his team into the workout area until he had everyone's attention, then he made sure that his team worked out in a professional manner with no sloppiness. Bela's stratagem worked, and later, when his team entered the gymnasium to compete for real, the crowd applauded mightily for the Romanians.

While performing on the uneven bars during the team competition on July 18, Nadia scored the first perfect 10 in Olympics history. The scoring apparatus was not programmed to display a score that high, so it displayed a 1.00, and gymnastics officials explained that it was really a 10. (For the next competition, the officials made sure to use a scoreboard that could display a perfect score of 10.) The Romanians won the silver medal, while the very strong Soviet team won the gold medal. Not until the 2000 Olympic Games in Sydney, Australia, would the Romanians defeat the Russians to win the Olympic gold medal in team competition. Previously to that, Romania won the gold medal in team competition at the 1984 Olympic Games, which was boycotted by the Soviets.

In individual competition, Nadia remained triumphant, winning gold in the all-around, balance beam, and uneven bars and a bronze in the floor exercise. During individual apparatus competition, Nadia earned perfect 10 scores on balance beam and uneven bars. By the time the Olympic Games were over, she had earned a total of seven perfect 10 scores. She earned four of the perfect scores on the uneven bars and three on the balance beam. Her performance caused television broadcaster Jim McKay to marvel that she was "swimming in an ocean of air."

Remarkably, Nadia seldom smiled or showed much emotion during competitions, in contrast to Olga Korbut, who had shown so much emotion—both happiness and grief—during the 1972 Olympic Games. Instead, Nadia concentrated on her performance as an athlete during competitions, and she smiled only after performing well on a piece of equipment or after winning a medal. Nadia explained, "I know how to smile, I know how to laugh, I know how to play. But I know how to do these things only after I have finished my mission."

One athlete who saw her at the Montreal Olympics in the dining hall was weightlifter Precious McKenzie of South Africa, who, like other athletes, wanted to see the tiny gymnast who was winning so many medals. He said, "She smiled, but she's a very shy little girl!" Nadia was such a celebrity that people were paying $100 for tickets that had originally cost $16 just so they could see her perform.

Lucky were the people who saw her. Nadia's gold medal in the all-around was a surprise to many gymnastics fans. Many people expected the gold medal to be won by one of the more experienced Soviet gymnasts: Nelli Kim, Olga Korbut, or Ludmilla Tourischeva. However, the Olympic Games have witnessed many displays of good sportsmanship. Soviet gymnasts Nelli Kim and Ludmilla Tourischeva are just two of the many Olympic champion athletes who have displayed such good sportsmanship. At the Montreal Olympic Games, Ludmilla settled for bronze as Nadia took the gold. Ludmilla wept when she realized that she had not repeated as Olympic all-around champion. Nevertheless, at the awards ceremony, Ludmilla shook young Nadia's hand and kissed her cheek. Nelli Kim, who won the silver, also shook Nadia's hand.

After winning the gold medal in the all-around, Nadia answered reporters' questions in a press conference. She told the reporters, "I was sure I would win. I knew that if I worked hard I would win." Nadia's French came in handy at the end of the Olympics when she said goodbye: "*Je remercie beaucoup la publique Canadienne.*" In English: "Again I thank the Canadian people very much." While in Montreal, she also bought a few dolls, explaining, "These will remind me of my seven 10's in the Olympics."

Some people at the Olympics questioned whether any gymnast could ever truly deserve a perfect score. In fact, one evening several fans yelled, "No more 10's! No more 10's!" American gymnast Cathy Rigby, who was the analyst for ABC, said about the judges, "They started out giving high scores, and Nadia is so superior to every girl here that they have no choice but to give her 10's." She was then asked, "In other words, if Nadia were competing against an abstract standard instead of human rivals, and if the crowd wasn't going wild, she might not get 10's?" Ms. Rigby thought for a moment, then replied, "If Nadia were doing what she's been doing, all alone in an empty room, I'd still have to say that she would get the 10's."

At Montreal, Nadia not only made history by earning the first-ever perfect 10 score in gymnastics at the Olympic Games, but she also introduced the Comaneci Salto. Because she was the first person to do this procedure in international competition, it is named after her. In addition, on the balance beam, she performed three back handsprings in a row. These feats made her an international celebrity. They also earned her such nicknames as "Miss Perfect

Ten," "The Gym Machine," "The Ice Queen," and "Little Miss Perfect." The last nickname made Nadia wish that people who called her that could see her grades on math exams. Of course, the name "Nadia" became famous, and in Montreal after the Olympics, over 150 families chose to name their newborn daughters Nadia after the young celebrity.

Sometimes it is difficult to be a young celebrity. When Nadia became the darling of the Montreal Olympics, she was asked the same questions many times by many journalists. Once, she complained, "It is harder for me to answer all these questions than to win a gold medal." She also pointed out, "I came here prepared to do gymnastics, not to be interviewed." One reporter actually asked her if she were going to retire after the Olympics! Nadia answered, "Retire? I am only fourteen years old." Twenty-five years after the Montreal Olympics, Nadia reflected on her reaction to her new celebrity status: "I was just a kid. I wanted to go home!"

Sometimes it is fun to be a young celebrity. When Nadia returned home to Romania, she was greeted by thousands of Romanians. A crowd of people sang, "Na-dia, Na-dia Comaneci, *Meritai si nota douazeci!*" ("Na-dia, Na-dia Comaneci, You deserved a twenty!"). This was fun, but one mishap caused her a problem—she explained to a reporter that she was "a little upset because one of my dolls lost its head in the plane." She also was thinking more about drinking some lemonade because she was hot than she was thinking about being a celebrity.

Nadia's victories were also victories for the Romanian people, and everyone celebrated with a parade. People made speeches and presentations in the Onesti sports arena, and large posters saying "Bravo, Nadia!" and bearing her portrait appeared on walls in Onesti. Of course, many people asked for her autograph. People even came to her house just so they could stand outside and look at the home of an Olympic champion.

On August 18, 1976, Nadia received the highest honor that the Romanian socialist government could bestow. In Bucharest (the capital of Romania), at a ceremony held in the Palace of Sports and Culture, she was given both the gold Hammer and Sickle Award and the title of Hero of Socialist Work. Nadia and her fellow gymnasts celebrated by performing a Romanian dance in traditional clothing. In addition, she appeared on an hour-long American television special titled *Nadia—from Romania with Love* with comedian Flip Wilson.

Chapter 4: After the Montreal Olympics

Late in 1976, the Romanian team visited Japan, where they became aware of one problem with success. The Romanian team's celebrity meant that many Japanese fans wanted to meet them, and when their plane landed in Tokyo, many people ran across the airfield to meet them. Some of the members of the team became separated from the other members, and mass confusion resulted. Finally, everyone was reunited and arrived safely at the hotel. No harm was done, but the team's hours for sightseeing and shopping were cancelled. This was a successful trip for the Romanians. Nadia won the Chunichi Cup, while her teammate and friend Teodora Ungureanu won the silver medal. In addition, both Nadia and Teodora, who was one year older minus a day, celebrated birthdays in Japan. Their Japanese hosts even made a birthday cake for their joint birthday party.

The Romanian women's gymnastics team went to West Germany in 1977 for a series of exhibitions. However, Romanian coach Bela Karolyi was very dissatisfied with the team's accommodations, which were not suitable for any team, much less a team that had won gold medals in the Olympics. Believe it or not, because of a mixup, the team was told to sleep in the freezing-cold changing room of the exhibition hall where they would soon display their skills! Bela even tried to get better accommodations by telling the exhibition hall manager that Nadia was feverish. However, instead of giving them better and warmer accommodations, the manager sent for a physician. When the physician arrived, Bela did not want him to examine Nadia and discover that she was not feverish, so she ran away from the physician. He chased her around the exhibition hall, but she kept eluding him, so eventually he gave up, saying, "If she can run like that, there can't be that much wrong with her, and if I can't examine her, what the hell can I do?"

Nadia expected to defend her American Cup title in 1977; however, a deadly earthquake struck Romania on March 4, killing more than 1,000 people. Instead of defending her title, Nadia and her teammates performed in exhibitions to raise money to help the victims of the earthquake.

Also in 1977, at the European Championships in Prague, Czechoslovakia, Nadia won the all-around. However, controversy arose during the individual events competition. Nadia tied for the gold medal in uneven bars, but in vault, a controversial judging decision awarded Nelli Kim the gold medal and Nadia the silver medal. Bela Karolyi protested, and Nicolae Ceauçescu, the dictator of Romania, ordered the team to leave the championships in protest. Because the team left the championships without permission from the head judge, Nadia was forced to give back her gold medal for the uneven bars. Bela blames the Romanian dictator for this misfortune. He believes that leaving the championships was an excessive reaction to the scoring controversy. He also believes that if the Romanians had been allowed to stay and compete, they could have won more gold medals.

Despite the judging controversy, Nadia won the all-around competition in the European Championships in 1977—and in 1979, becoming the first woman to win it three times. (She had also won it in 1975.) Each time, she was coached by Bela, although part of the time between 1977 and 1979 she was coached by someone else.

Despite Nadia's success, in early 1977, Bela Karolyi was removed as Nadia's coach. The reasons given for the removal of Bela as Nadia's coach vary. According to Bela, the coaching change was motivated by jealousy of his success in the Romanian coaching establishment. When his gymnasts were removed to Bucharest, he wasn't even told. Instead, he arrived at the gym for a training session only to find that it was empty! A rival coach of Bela's was now training his gymnasts in the Romanian capital city.

According to Nadia's autobiography, *Nadia*, there were some tensions between her and Bela. As a girl growing into a woman, Nadia wanted more freedom, but as a coach, Bela wanted her to train hard and maintain a competitive weight, two things which require close supervision. Unfortunately, even after leaving Bela for another coach, Nadia still suffered from a lack of freedom—top athletes in socialist countries tend to be carefully watched by a wide assortment of people, including coaches, physicians, choreographers, and nutritionists, who try to ensure that the athletes stay in top athletic condition. Perhaps both explanations are true.

In the meantime, Bela moved from Onesti to Deva, where he successfully coached other young gymnasts, including Daniela Silivas. His new young gymnasts even won a national championship over his old gymnasts who were no longer training with him!

Following the removal of Bela as her head coach, Nadia ran into difficulties. She entered puberty, a time of rapid growth that can throw off an athlete's abilities. She grew four inches, and she gained a lot of weight, some of it from poor eating habits. At a 1977 exhibition, Nadia gave American gymnast Jackie Cassello a $20 bill, then whispered to her, "Chocolates, doughnuts, Cokes, candy bars …." Adding to Nadia's difficulties in 1977, her parents decided to divorce.

The year 1978 was also difficult for Nadia. She supposedly drank some bleach and was hospitalized in what was widely called a suicide attempt; however, in her autobiography titled *Nadia*, which she actually may not have had much to do with, she explained that it was an accident. On a desk she had a cup of bleach because she was going to wash her clothing. She also had a cup of fruit juice. Upset following an argument about her lack of freedom, she reached for the cup of fruit juice, accidentally picked up the cup of bleach instead, and swallowed some of it before she realized her mistake. Fortunately, she recovered. Other people, including Bela, said that it was a suicide attempt.

In Nadia's most recent autobiography, *Letters to a Young Gymnast*, which is definitely hers, she flatly denies that she ever drank bleach and that she ever tried to commit suicide. Instead, she writes that she was doing her laundry and she was upset at her lack of personal freedom—as a Communist country, Romania had secret police and other officials who kept a close eye on the citizens, including citizens who were elite athletes. When a spy—uh, official—asked Nadia where she was going, she complained, "What are you doing here? Why can't I do laundry without the third degree? How can I feel relaxed when there are people ready to jump on me at every corner? Maybe I should just drink this bottle of beach and commit suicide. Please leave me alone!" Nadia writes that the rumor that she had tried to commit suicide arose from this flippant remark.

Fortunately, Nadia and Bela were reunited in time for the 1978 World Championships, the 1979 European Championships, and the 1979 World Championships. Their reunion led to great success for both of them after a somewhat shaky start.

In 1978, at the World Championships in Strasbourg, France, Nadia placed a disappointing fourth in the all-around after a fall on the uneven bars. According to Bela, when Nadia began training with him, she was fat and out of shape, but she worked hard and lost most of the 40 pounds she had gained. Losing the weight was difficult, partly because Nadia had a secret source supplying her with chocolate—but Bela stopped the secret source. Because of her hard work and Bela's coaching, she won the gold medal on the balance beam. As a team, the Romanians won the silver medal.

In 1979, at the European Championships in Oslo, Norway, Nadia was back in shape, having lost all the weight she had gained while Bela was not coaching her. She won the European all-around competition for the third time, becoming the first woman gymnast to do so.

Also in 1979, with Bela as her head coach, Nadia led the Romanian team to its first-ever team gold medal at the World Championships in Fort Worth, Texas. She led the competition after the compulsories, but then she developed a cellulitis infection in her wrist after accidentally scratching it with the buckle on a pair of hand guards. Because of this, she had an operation on her inflamed wrist. According to Bela, this operation was completely unnecessary—the "cellulitis infection" was nothing more than a scratch, which he treated with an antibiotic cream and then bandaged. Bela believes that the opening of the wrist and the stitches were ordered by a Romanian gymnastics rival who was jealous of Bela's success.

Because of Nadia's operation, instead of having six gymnasts competing and being able to drop the lowest score, the Romanians had to compete with only five gymnasts and count all their scores. At first, all went well. The Romanians scored high on the uneven bars, including some perfect scores—9.8, 9.9, 10, 10, 10. Nadia merely touched the uneven bars and did not perform her routine. But disaster struck on the balance beam. The first four gymnasts performed well, but the fifth gymnast fell off the beam, greatly lowering her score. It seemed as if the Soviet team had won yet another team World Championship gold medal.

However, realizing that her team needed her to perform on balance beam so that the Romanians could drop the score of the gymnast who fell, Nadia accepted the challenge. Being careful to protect her injured wrist, she performed the exercise almost one-handed, although blood could be seen seeping through her bandage. She scored 9.95, enough to give the Romanians the victory, but she was not able to compete in the individual events following the team competition. In his autobiography titled *Feel No Fear*, Bela writes that Nadia "had made her contribution to the team's victory. What she did not realize at the time was that she had just written an unforgettable page in the history of gymnastics about courage, dedication, and the spirit of sacrifice of a young human being."

Chapter 5: The 1980 Olympic Games

Early in 1980, Nadia stopped training with Bela Karolyi for a while and moved to Bucharest, then returned to him to train for the Olympics. After training with Bela, Nadia won more medals at the 1980 Olympic Games in Moscow, despite suffering from sciatica, which made her legs ache.

The gold medal for the all-around competition went to the Soviets' Elena Davidova in a controversial decision. Bela charged that Nadia lost the gold medal in the all-around competition due to biased, politically motivated judging. Indeed, according to Bela, the Olympics were stacked against the Romanians. For one thing, the stands were filled with Russian soldiers who booed the tiny Romanian gymnasts. In his autobiography titled *Feel No Fear*, Bela wrote that he felt like telling them, "These are just young ladies and you are hurting them. Hurt me, don't hurt my kids."

After a delay of nearly 30 minutes, the judges gave Nadia a score of 9.85 for her final routine on the balance beam. The score allowed the Soviet Union's Yelena Davydova to win the gold medal by .075 of a point. Nadia tied Maxi Gnauck of the German Democratic Republic for the silver medal.

According to Bela, judges from Bulgaria, Czechoslovakia, Poland, and the Soviet Union originally gave Nadia scores that would have given Nadia the gold medal. However, Bela said, the head of the technical committee of the women's gymnastics federation ordered the lowering of the marks, thus giving Yelena the gold medal.

This charge has been denied. The official explanation is that the Romanian head judge challenged the scores given by the judges from Bulgaria, Czechoslovakia, Poland, and the Soviet Union, the judges debated the scores, and the scores remained unchanged. Therefore, according to the official explanation of the judges' decision, Yelena deserved her gold medal.

Bela strongly disagrees. Each time the scoreboard gave Nadia a score of 9.85, he knocked it down. According to Bela, the judges had deliberately made Nadia wait to compete on her final event, the balance beam, until Yelena had finished competing on her final event, the uneven bars, so that they would know what score to give Nadia to ensure that she came in second.

Twenty years after she won the all-around gold medal in 1980, Yelena said that she is disappointed that some people think her victory was a fluke. She said, "Everyone works hard, but only one person wins. Some people are in better shape at the time, some fall, some are sick. Even at the 2000 Olympics, a lot of girls could have won, but only one did. A lot of gymnasts deserved to do well, but only one finished on top."

Nevertheless, Nadia won gold medals in the balance beam—scoring a perfect 10 her first time up in the team competition—and floor exercise, and silver medals in the team competition and in the all-around.

Because of Nadia's success as a gymnast in high profile events such as the Olympic Games, the Romanian government allowed her to live much better than other Romanians. The government gave her an eight-room villa and an automobile with a license plate with only three digits. The three digits indicated that Nadia had the government's permission to drive as fast as she wanted.

Chapter 6: Retirement, Defection, and Marriage

In 1981, Nadia competed in her final major competition, the World University Games, which were held in Bucharest, Romania. She won all the gold medals, coming in first in all-around, balance beam, floor exercise, uneven bars, and vault. However, the scoring for the competition was questionable, as some people felt that the scoring for Nadia was lenient.

Also in 1981, her coaches, Bela Karolyi and his wife, Marta, defected from Romania to the United States. The defection occurred during a tour of the United States by members of the Romanian gymnastics team, including Nadia. One of the reasons Bela and Marta gave for their defection was that Romanian authorities continually interfered with the way they trained their gymnasts, including Nadia. In addition, Bela was in disgrace with the Romanian socialist government because of the way he had protested what he called biased scoring at the 1980 Olympic Games in Moscow. Nadia wanted to defect, too, when she learned of the Karolyis' plans, but Bela knew that defection would lead to hard times as they adjusted to life in a new country, so he persuaded her that it was not the right time for her to defect.

Following their defection, the Karolyis' life was hard, as they learned how to speak English by watching such television programs as *Sesame Street*. However, they received help from such people as Les Sasvary, the vice president of the United States Gymnastics Federation; Texas congressman Bill Archer, who helped them bring their daughter, Andrea, to the United States; and from Paul Ziert (the coach of Bart Conner), who helped them get jobs.

With this help and with the help of their own hard work, the Karolyis were able to succeed in America. The Karolyis began coaching again, taking Mary Lou Retton to Olympic gold in the all-around in 1984 and taking the USA women's gymnastics team to team gold in 1996.

The Karolyis have a 1,200-acre ranch in the Sam Houston National Forest in Texas, where they also run a gymnastics camp. The ranch is filled with animals, including a camel, ducks, an emu, flamingos, horses, llamas, ostriches, and swans, as well as numerous dogs. Bela enjoys hunting, and among his trophies is a mounted moose head bearing a 63-inch rack. He shot the moose in Alaska in 1987.

A movie titled *Nadia* was made about her life in 1984, but she received no money from it. According to Nadia, "I think it's a pretty good movie. I didn't even know that there was a movie about me. What I like is that a lot of things with my gymnastics in the movie [are] not always good. [Viewers] see the mistakes. [Viewers] see me falling on the beam. So little girls say, 'Oh, Nadia falls, too.' And they know it's OK to make mistakes."

Following her retirement from gymnastics competition in 1984, Nadia became a coach for the Romanian junior national team and also served as a gymnastics judge. However, the Romanian socialist government at that time was repressive and following her retirement greatly restricted her travel abroad. However, the Romanian government did allow her to travel to two Olympic Games.

At the time, Romania was still a Communist country and since much of its food was exported, food for its own citizens could be rare, even for people such as Nadia Comaneci, after she retired from gymnastics. She had an old neighbor, around 70 years old, named Aleca Petre, who would get up early at 4 a.m., then stand in line during cold winter weather to get into a grocery store to see what food was on the shelves. According to Nadia, most of the time only beans, mustard, and mayonnaise were on the shelves. However, he would bring her milk when he could—and sometimes even some meat. Nadia points out that Romanians were always willing to share what food they had. She says, "That is the way Romanians are: We share what we have."

Even when Nadia was still competing, the Romanian government had been repressive and had watched her, afraid that she would defect. After all, many other Romanians had defected. The Romanian government continued to watch her after she retired from competition. During a 1984 interview with an ABC reporter in Los Angeles, Nadia at first was at ease and answered questions freely. However, suddenly she became nervous and gave halting answers to the reporter's questions because she had glimpsed a member of the Romanian Securitate (police) nearby, watching her.

Shortly before Nadia defected, the Romanian government had been offered $100,000 to let Nadia go on tour in the United States with gymnasts Olga Korbut and Mary Lou Retton. Ironically, the Romanian government declined the offer because of the fear that she would defect during the tour.

On the night of November 27, 1989, at the age of 28, Nadia defected from Romania. She didn't even tell her parents that she was defecting—"I was afraid they'd have a heart attack." She and six others walked six hours, taking with them only what they could carry, waded icy rivers, and crossed the border—patrolled by armed guards—into Hungary. The most valuable thing Nadia carried was the denim jacket she wore. In addition, she wore a backpack. She said, "It was very difficult leaving my family and friends behind, knowing that if the political system in Romania didn't change, I would never see them again."

In addition to leaving her family and friends behind, Nadia also left behind all of her medals. As soon as the Romanian government learned that Nadia had defected, dictator Nicolae Ceauçescu sent people to get her medals from her home. However, Nadia had so many medals—150 to 200—that they weren't able to move them right away. Before they could move them, the revolution broke out and Ceauçescu was executed. Nadia's brother kept the medals for her, and when he visited her, he brought the medals with him. Today, Nadia keeps her Olympic medals in a bank vault.

After crossing the Romanian border, Nadia then made her way to Vienna, Austria, where the United States Embassy granted her political asylum. From there, she went to North America. When she landed at JFK Airport in New York, she told reporters why she had defected, saying, "I wanted to have a free life."

Many Romanians also wanted to have a free life. The government of Romanian dictator Nicolae Ceauçescu had grown more and more repressive, even as other countries in Eastern Europe were gaining more freedom. In fact, in 1988, the United States withdrew Romania's status as a Most Favored Nation for trade purposes because of the numerous human rights violations committed by Ceauçescu's repressive government.

Following her defection was a bad time for Nadia. The man who had helped her to defect turned out not to be a nice man. In his hands, she was almost a prisoner. She performed at gymnastics exhibitions and gave interviews for money, but he kept all the money she made. In addition, she acquired bad eating habits as a result of the stress she was under. While she was living in south Florida, a bartender named Cathy Campbell got to know her and told the *Fort Lauderdale News and Sun-Sentinel*, "She eats five times a day." Several media reports focused on the huge amounts of food she was eating shortly after arriving in the United States.

Fortunately, she received help from American gymnast Bart Conner, from her former coach Bela Karolyi, and from Montreal-based physical therapist Alexandru Stefu, who had been a rugby coach when he lived in Romania.

When Bart saw in a listing of TV shows that Nadia was scheduled to appear on *The Pat Sajak Show* on January 13, 1990, he used his fame as an Olympic gold medal-winning American gymnast to talk himself onto the show. (Bart had won two gold medals at the 1984 Olympic Games in Los Angeles—team and parallel bars.) He called Michael Weisman, the show's executive producer, who invited him to appear on the show as long as he could be in Los Angeles by 5 p.m.

Bart made sure that he appeared on the show and met Nadia. He said, "I grabbed the cellular phone, jumped in a cab, flew to LA, changed clothes in the bathroom of the plane—which only a gymnast can do—and was picked up by a helicopter." By the time he reached the show, Nadia was already on the air. Bart was handed two dozen roses, which he presented to Nadia, saying, "Welcome to America."

On *The Pat Sajak Show*, Bart became acquainted again with Nadia. He also discovered that she was afraid of the man who had helped her escape from Romania. He said, "I knew she needed help." Although Bart gave her his telephone number, Nadia was still unable to get away from the man who was keeping her a virtual prisoner.

So why didn't she call the police to free her from the man? She said, "I was afraid of him. I could never defend myself because I never had a minute away from him. I didn't go to the police because in Romania the police are the bad guys." The man controlled her actions and wouldn't even let her answer the telephone.

Part of the reason for her inability to leave him was psychological. Because she had grown up in a socialist country, Nadia was unused to freedom, and she didn't know that she could leave. She said, "I was afraid. I couldn't even call my mom. She thought I was dead because the paper said I was shot at the border." Nadia was also afraid that the man would return her to Romania. Several times, he threatened to take her back unless she did as he said.

Understandably, Nadia says little today about this bad time in her life. Fortunately, her story has a happy ending.

Her former coach Bela Karolyi knew Alexandru Stefu and urged him to contact and help Nadia. Alexandru lured the man who had been keeping Nadia a virtual prisoner for three months into a meeting in Los Angeles to discuss a possible money-making deal in Canada. Alexandru was not able to see Nadia alone, but from her body language he knew that something was wrong. He convinced the man to bring Nadia to Montreal, and finally he was able to talk to her alone. Nadia told Alexandru that the man was mistreating her. She said, "This is a bad guy. Please help me." Realizing that the truth was known, the man fled, stealing $150,000 of her money and her Mercedes.

However, in her autobiography titled *Letters to a Young Gymnast*, Nadia does not speak badly of the man who helped her defect from Romania. She writes about him, "I never heard from him again, but I hope he is well and thank him for his help."

For 18 months, Nadia lived in a second-floor apartment above Alexandru and his family. During the time that

Nadia spent living with Alexandru's family, she and Bart Conner became telephone pals. One day, after yet another telephone conversation, Bart hung up, and then he realized, "My God, I'm falling in love."

In 1991, Alexandru died in a freak accident in his swimming pool, so Nadia called Bart for help. Bart said, "I'd never heard anyone so terrified in my life. Stefu was the one good thing that had happened to her life [since her defection] and he was gone." Nadia moved to Norman, Oklahoma, where she trained under coach Paul Ziert, and where she renewed her acquaintance with Bart.

After coming to live in the United States, Nadia enjoyed watching television. Like many other women, she became addicted to a favorite soap opera—one that she referred to, because of difficulty with the English language, as *The Young and the Wrestlers*. Actually, Nadia is quite good with languages. In addition to Romanian and English, she speaks French, Italian, and Spanish.

In the early 1990s, Nadia and Bart performed at many gymnastics exhibitions together, and they fell in love. Nadia and Bart decided to visit Romania together in 1994, her first visit to her native country since she had defected. While they were traveling to Romania, he proposed to her on November 12 (her 33rd birthday) at the Amsteel International Hotel in Amsterdam, surprising her with a 3.3-carat engagement ring that he had designed himself. Bart said, "She was so surprised, I had to ask her again."

Nadia admits that the proposal was a surprise—partly because she had expected him to propose a couple of years earlier. However, the proposal wasn't entirely unexpected. Nadia said, "He got me a ring, then a bracelet—he was running out of jewelry. The engagement ring had to be next." Before Bart proposed to her, Nadia had a hint that it was about to happen—three hours before they were to go out, he started dressing. Her acceptance of his proposal made Bart so happy that he left a big—uh, make that *huge*—tip at the restaurant they ate at that evening.

When they reached Romania, Bart asked Nadia's father for permission to marry her. Her father readily consented to the wedding, saying in Romanian, "With all my heart." He also reminisced about what Nadia had been like as a child, when she used to bounce on the furniture: "I remember when she used to break all the mattresses."

Because Nadia is such a national hero of Romania, it's as if she belongs to everyone there. Bart even said that "the running joke over there was that I should ask the president and prime minister about marrying her."

On Friday, April 26, 1996, at the invitation of Romania's president and prime minister, Nadia and Bart were married in Bucharest, Romania. Bart was 38, and Nadia was 34. The wedding was a civil ceremony in the Army Club. It was carried live on Romanian television, and fans watched the wedding outside on a huge television screen. The following day highlights were shown on American television on ABC's *Wide World of Sports*.

Nadia wore a white wedding dress embroidered with white roses, and she had six attendants to carry her 23-foot-long train. The $50,000 dress was designed by Yumi Katsura of Japan. Bart wore a black morning jacket, a white shirt with a white bowtie, and white gloves. For the wedding and reception, Bart learned to speak some Romanian. Fortunately, for the wedding ceremony, he needed to learn only one word of Romanian—*da*, meaning "yes" or "I do."

After the wedding, Bart and Nadia went out on a balcony to address the people outside. From the balcony, Bart used his

Romanian language skills to give a short speech in which he said, "Thank you for accepting me."

The next day, Nadia and Bart were wedded again—this time in a church. Seven priests, including Bishop Teofan, assistant to the archbishop of Romania, blessed the union in Bucharest's Casin Orthodox monastery. Both Bart and Nadia wore the traditional Orthodox gold crowns. Outside the church, 2,000 spectators watched, while inside the church, 150 guests witnessed the wedding. One of the guests was Paul Ziert, who cried with happiness. Family attended the wedding, including the parents and brothers of both Nadia and Bart.

At the Orthodox church wedding, Nadia ground her heel onto Bart's foot. This was not an accident. Bart explains that according to Romanian culture, "If the woman stomps on your foot, she establishes her power in the relationship for the rest of your life." Nadia also kept her maiden name after the wedding.

When most people speculate about the happiest time of Nadia's life, they probably think of her performance at the 1976 Olympic Games in Montreal. In fact, on the last day of competition at the Montreal Olympics, after she had won five medals, Nadia said, "Today is the happiest day of my life!" However, on the day of her wedding, Nadia said, "Today, the 1976 Montreal Olympics move on to second place for me."

Bart referred to their marriage as a union between "Joe Midwest and the mysterious beauty from Transylvania." (Transylvania, where the fictional vampire Dracula is from, is in Romania.) Bart also said, "Most guys brag that their wives are a 10. My wife is the 10."

Following the church wedding, the president of Romania, Ion Iliescu, hosted a reception for them in the main hall of

Cotroceni Palace. Bart and Nadia then honeymooned in Greece.

Chapter 7: Nadia's Life More Recently

When Nadia and Bart are together, people often recognize Bart first. Many fans remember Nadia as the 14-year-old girl who weighed 86 pounds and stood not quite five feet tall at the 1976 Olympic Games in Montreal. Because the United States boycotted the 1980 Olympic Games in the Soviet Union, few people in the West saw the 18-year-old, grown-up Nadia compete.

Although most Americans still think of Nadia as the 14-year-old darling of the Montreal Olympics, of course she is an adult woman today. According to Nadia, "It seems like everybody knows I was 14 in 1976. It's terrible. I'll never be able to lie about my age."

Of course, she is a sports celebrity, and other gymnasts and gymnastics fans ask her for her autograph; however, Nadia suspects what may actually be happening when very young gymnasts ask her to sign something: "Their mothers remember me." Today, she receives mail that is addressed with these few words, "Nadia, Oklahoma, USA."

In 1997, Nadia was traveling on an airplane when a flight attendant noticed her muscular legs and asked if she were an athlete. Nadia replied that she was a gymnast, and the flight attendant joked, "Who do you think you are—Nadia Comaneci?" Nadia replied, "Well, I am," startling the flight attendant so much that she spilled coffee on Nadia's shirt. Nadia did not get upset, but simply changed her shirt in the airplane restroom. She also autographed the coffee-stained shirt and gave it to the flight attendant.

As sports celebrities, Nadia and Bart have had many interesting experiences. In 1992, they led the contestants of the Miss USA beauty pageant through a series of exercises. At the end of the workout, Bart said there was one more optional exercise left, then he grinned and performed a back flip. None of the Miss USA contestants did the optional exercise. Bart and Nadia once appeared on TV's *Hollywood Squares* together. They admitted that it was tough to be a married couple who had to sit in a box together and reach agreement on their answers while hundreds of thousands of Americans watched them. In January 2002, they carried the Olympic torch through Oklahoma City as it made its way to Salt Lake City for the Winter Olympics.

Currently, Nadia is a contributing editor of *International Gymnast* magazine, and Bart is associate publisher. (Paul Ziert is publisher.) Nadia occasionally contributes articles to the magazine, including interviews with such stars of gymnastics as Romania's Alexandra Marinescu, and she and Bart have written such continuing features as *Training Tips* and *Ask Bart and Nadia*. For a while, they also starred in a cable TV show titled *Food and Fitness*, which featured nutritious recipes. Bart also produces sports shows for television with his production company, which he has named Perfect 10 Productions.

Nadia and Bart also own a 26,000-square-foot gymnasium—Bart Conner's Gymnastics Academy—in Norman, Oklahoma, where they coach. The gymnastics school has over 25 certified instructors. In August of 1999, 13 gymnasts from Norman, Oklahoma, traveled with Nadia to Romania to train.

In addition, Nadia and Bart contribute time and money to charitable organizations. In particular, they support children's charities such as the Special Olympics and the Muscular Dystrophy Association. In fact, in 1982, Bart appeared on the Jerry Lewis Labor Day Telethon, where he gave Mr. Lewis—who was wearing a tuxedo—lessons on the pommel horse. In addition, they support the Canadian

Quebec Agency, which advocates the adoption of Romanian children.

Bart got Nadia involved in working with the Muscular Dystrophy Association. Before hosting the MDA telethon in Chicago, he suggested that she call and make a pledge. She did call, but when she said, "I'm Nadia Comaneci," the woman who had answered the telephone said, "I'm Queen Elizabeth," then hung up. Nadia called again, and this time the woman told Bart that a woman who called herself Nadia Comaneci was on the telephone and he replied that he was expecting her to call.

The year 2001 was a good year for Nadia. Her Romanian teammate in Montreal, Teodora Ungureanu, was inducted into the International Gymnastics Hall of Fame in Oklahoma City, Oklahoma. In Montreal, Teodora had won two silvers and a bronze. Nadia was present for the ceremony, and the two got to talk face to face about old times.

On June 29, 2001, Nadia reached another milestone in her life—she became a citizen of the United States. Along with 180 other immigrants, she took the oath for citizenship at the federal courthouse in Oklahoma City. Bart was present, busily taking photographs.

At the ceremony, Nadia served as guest speaker, saying, "This is a great day for all of us here. America is a nation of immigrants. We must celebrate our diversity." She added, "We must never take our freedom for granted. As new citizens, we must discover where we can make a contribution to America, and where we can make a difference."

Of course, Bart is very proud that his wife has become an American citizen. On the day she received her citizenship, he said, "I'm thrilled. This is a great, great day for us."

Actually, Nadia is now a citizen of two countries, as she has retained her citizenship in her native Romania. Nadia supports the Romanian Gymnastics Federation and the gymnastics school named after her in Onesti, Romania, where she was born. Over the years, she has donated over $100,000 to the Romanian national gymnastics team. She said, "Even though I live full-time in the U.S., I love to travel to Romania as often as I can to support my family, friends, and the Romanian gymnastics program."

In addition, Nadia has business interests there. In March 2001 she opened a sports bar named Champions in Bucharest. Sports memorabilia is displayed, and the servers are dressed as referees in T-shirts with black and white stripes. Of course, she also endorses many companies and products, such as Danskin, which makes women's tights.

Nadia stays in shape and works out at a health club with weights. Often, she works out in health clubs in hotels because she spends so much time traveling. She also does gymnastics, but only easy skills. In 2001, she turned 40, but her work with weights and exercise have paid off. According to Nadia, "I feel better at 40 than I did at 30." She also said, "I used to think 40 was old, but I don't feel that right now, because I look in the mirror and I like what I see." In addition, she maintains contact with old friends, including Bela Karolyi, her Olympic coach. According to Nadia, "Seeing him always brings back memories. He's always going to be a big part of my life; I don't care if he moves to Alaska."

On June 3, 2006, Nadia reached another milestone in her life when she gave birth to Dylan Paul Conner, her and Bart's first child. The nurses in the hospital at Oklahoma City put up a poster announcing that Dylan Paul was "a perfect 10."

Like many busy, famous people, Bart and Nadia waited until later in life to have their child, and sometimes they joke that when their son loses his baby teeth, they will need dentures. In fact, Bart says, "We're also joking that by the time he's out of diapers, we'll be going into them." However, Nadia demurs, "He meant, *Bart* will be going into them."

Dylan Paul will be the Conners' only child. Nadia says about childbearing, "I'm done."

In other family news, Nadia's father, Gheorghe, retired from his job as a car mechanic. He never owned a car, preferring to walk 12 miles to and from his job each day. Why? He explains that cars always break down. Now, he has a small business of his own: He sells his own pickled vegetables in a farmer's market. These days, because he works for himself, Nadia calls him "Mr. President."

So how does Nadia sum up her life, which was not always happy, but which is happy now? According to Nadia, "Looking back, I wouldn't change anything at all about my life including the difficulties I lived through. Without my past I wouldn't be where I am today. It's been like a fairy tale ...."

Chapter 8: Legacy and Accomplishments

The two gymnasts who have popularized women's gymnastics the most throughout the world have been Olga Korbut and Nadia Comaneci. Although Nadia rarely smiled or showed emotion while competing, due to her concentration, crowds fell in love with her during the major impact she made during the 1976 Olympic Games, just as they had earlier when Olga Korbut, who did show emotion while competing, made a major impact during the 1972 Olympic Games. Together, Nadia and Olga made women's gymnastics the premier event at the Summer Olympics and both have influenced many young girls to take up the sport of gymnastics.

One such girl was Mary Lou Retton. When she was eight years old, Mary Lou watched on TV as Nadia won medal after medal at the 1976 Olympics. Mary Lou told her mother, "Mom, I want to be just like Nadia, and I want to be in the Olympics." Her mother did what any mother would do, and replied, "Sure, honey, sure." At the 1984 Olympics, Mary Lou won the gold medal in the all-around competition.

It took a while for Mary Lou to become that good. When she competed for the first time as a very young gymnast in Parkersburg, West Virginia, she fell off the beam a few times and was spotted by her coach constantly throughout her routine. The judges awarded her a 1, but young Mary Lou thought she had gotten a perfect score of 10, because Nadia had gotten a 10 at the Olympics, and since the Olympics scoring apparatus wasn't programmed to go that high, it had displayed the numeral 1.

Of course, Nadia influenced many other girls' decisions to become gymnasts. In Nadia's native Romania, Daniela Silivas watched the 1976 Olympic Games on television.

After witnessing Nadia's perfect scores, Daniela decided to go into gymnastics. She even earned some perfect scores of her own. The first came in Montreal, where Nadia had earned so many perfect scores. Daniela won a gold medal with a perfect 10 on balance beam at the 1985 World Championships.

One non-famous athlete inspired by Nadia is Caitlin Chambers, who lives in Florida, has Down syndrome, and participates in the Special Olympics. Her specialty is cartwheels, and she says that she decided to become a gymnast after watching such athletes as Nadia and American gymnast Dominique Dawes, who won a team gold medal at the 1996 Olympic Games in Atlanta.

Nadia does much motivational speaking, and she advises young gymnasts, "If you go for a little gold every day instead of saving that energy for a big championship, that's the best way. You have to say, 'Let's see what I can do tomorrow better than I did today.'" And she advises young women, "Go in any direction you want to go. If you want to accomplish something, you can. It may not be easy work, but you have to believe in it and not give up."

Throughout her career, Nadia has won many honors and awards. In 1993, she was inducted into the International Gymnastics Hall of Fame.

In 1998, she won the Flo Hyman award, which is "presented to the athlete who exemplifies the same dignity, spirit, and commitment to excellence as the late Flo Hyman, captain of the 1984 U.S. Olympic volleyball team."

As you would expect, at the turn of the millennium, Nadia was named to many all-century teams and won many honors. For example, *Real Sport* magazine selected her as one of the top five women athletes of the century. In

Vienna, Austria, at the World Sports awards, Nadia was named one of the athletes of the century. Other athletes named included Muhammad Ali, Steffi Graf, Carl Lewis, and Pele. In 1999, the International Association of Sports Writers voted her one of the outstanding sports people of the century. In addition, a *Sports Illustrated* 16-member panel put her 52nd in a list of the 100 greatest athletes of the twentieth century.

Nadia's accomplishments are many, with the gymnastics high point being her performance at the 1976 Olympics in Montreal. She ended her Olympics career with 5 gold medals, 3 silver medals, and 1 bronze medal. In addition, during her career, she scored a perfect 10 a total of 31 times.

When he was the president of the United States Gymnastics Federation, Frank Bare said, "There is always the challenge in gymnastics to do something nobody has done before."

Nadia met that challenge.

Appendix A: Chronology

November 12, 1961

• Nadia Comaneci is born in Onesti, Romania.

1968

• Nadia begins training with coach Bela Karolyi.

1975

• At the European championships, Nadia wins gold in the all-around, balance beam, uneven parallel bars, and vault. In the remaining event, the floor exercise, she wins silver.

1976

• Nadia wins the American Cup with several perfect 10 scores.

• At the Olympic Games in Montreal, Nadia earns the first perfect 10 score in Olympics history. She earns perfect 10's on the balance beam and uneven bars. Her medals are gold in all-around, balance beam, and uneven bars, silver in team, and bronze in floor exercise. She receives seven perfect 10 scores in all. At this competition, she becomes the first person to perform the Salto Comaneci in international competition; because of this, the maneuver is named after her.

• Nadia is named the 1976 ABC Wide World of Sports Athlete of the Year.

• Nadia is given the Hero of Socialist Work award, becoming the youngest Romanian to be given the award.

1977

• An earthquake hits Romania; Nadia and her teammates perform at exhibitions to raise money to help the victims of the earthquake.

• At the European Championships in Prague, Czechoslovakia, Nadia wins the all-around. However, Nadia is forced to give back her gold medal for the uneven bars after the Romanian team leaves to protest what it feels is unfair judging.

• Bela Karolyi temporarily ceases to be Nadia's coach.

1978

• Nadia supposedly drinks some bleach in what is either an accident or a suicide attempt; however, she may not have drunk bleach at all.

• Bela Karolyi is reinstated as Nadia's coach.

• At the World Championships in Strasbourg, France, Nadia places a disappointing fourth in the all-around after a fall on the uneven bars; however, she wins the gold medal on the balance beam. As a team, the Romanians win the silver medal.

1979

• Nadia leads the Romanian team to its first-ever team gold medal at the World Championships despite having an inflamed wrist.

• Nadia wins the all-around gold medal at the European Championships, becoming the first person to win it three times. (She also won it in 1975 and 1977.)

1980

• At the Olympic Games in Moscow, which the Americans boycotted, Nadia wins gold in balance beam and floor exercise (a tie), and silver in all-around (a tie) and team.

1981

• Nadia competes in her final major competition, the World University Games, which were held in Bucharest, Romania. She wins all the gold medals, coming in first in all-around, balance beam, floor exercise, uneven bars, and vault.

• Bela and Marta Karolyi defect from Romania to the United States.

1984

• The TV movie titled *Nadia* is made about her life.

• Nadia officially retires from gymnastics competition.

November 27, 1989

• Nadia defects from Romania and then comes to the United States.

1990

• Nadia is rescued by Alexandru Stefu from the man who had kept her almost a hostage.

• Nadia is inducted into the Sudafed International Women's Sports Hall of Fame.

1993

• Nadia is inducted into the International Gymnastics Hall of Fame.

November 12, 1994

• American gymnast Bart Conner proposes to Nadia on her 33rd birthday at the Amsteel International Hotel in Amsterdam.

April 26, 1996

• Nadia marries Bart Conner.

1998

• Nadia is given the Flo Hymen Award.

2000

• In Vienna, Austria, at the World Sports awards, Nadia is named one of the Athletes of the Century. Other athletes named include Muhammad Ali, Steffi Graf, Carl Lewis, and Pele.

June 29, 2001

• Nadia becomes a citizen of the United States; she has dual citizenship in the United States and in Romania.

2004

• Nadia publishes *Letters to a Young Gymnast*.

June 3, 2006

• Nadia gives birth to Dylan Paul Conner, her and Bart's first and only child.

Appendix B: Book Bibliography

Reference Works

Christensen, Karen, Allen Guttmann, and Gertrud Pfister, editors. *International Encyclopedia of Women and Sports*. New York: Macmillan Reference USA, 2001.

Editors of Salem Press. *Great Athletes*. Pasadena, CA: Salem Press, Inc., 2002.

Hasday, Judy L. *Extraordinary Women Athletes*. New York: Children's Press, 2000.

Johnson, Anne Janette. *Great Women in Sports*. Detroit, MI: Visible Ink Press, 1996.

Layden, Joseph. *Women in Sports: The Complete Book on the World's Greatest Female Athletes*. Los Angeles, CA: General Publishing Group, 1997.

Markel, Robert, executive editor. *The Women's Sports Encyclopedia*. Susan Waggoner, managing editor; Marcella Smith, research and records editor. New York: Henry Holt and Company, 1997.

McGovern, Michael. *The Encyclopedia of Twentieth-Century Athletes*. New York: Facts on File, 2001.

Oglesby, Carole A., editor. *Encyclopedia of Women and Sport in America*. Phoenix, AZ: Oryx Press, 1998.

Woolum, Janet. *Outstanding Women Athletes*. Phoenix, AZ: Oryx Press, 1992.

Books for Young Readers

Burchard, S. H. *Nadia Comaneci*. New York: Harcourt Brace Jovanovich, 1977.

Green, Septima. *Top 10 Women Gymnasts*. Berkeley Heights, NJ: Enslow Publications, Inc., 1999.

Jones, Betty Milsaps. *Wonder Women of Sports*. New York: Random House, 1981.

Meyer, Miriam Weiss, project editor. *Top Picks: People*. Pleasantville, New York: Reader's Digest Educational Division, 1977.

Sorensen, Robert. *Shadow of the Past: True Life Sports Stories.* Middletown, CT: Xerox Education Publications, 1978.

Sullivan, George. *The Picture Story of Nadia Comaneci.* New York: Julian Messner, 1977.

Books for Teenagers and Adults

Comaneci, Nadia. *Letters to a Young Gymnast.* New York: Basic Books, 2004.

Comaneci, Nadia. *Nadia: The Autobiography of Nadia Comaneci.* London: Proteus Books, 1981.

Connock, Marion. *Nadia of Romania.* London: Gerald Duckworth and Co., Ltd., 1977.

Frist, Karyn McLaughlin, editor. *"Love You, Daddy Boy": Daughters Honor the Fathers They Love.* Lanham, MD: Taylor Trade Publishing, 2006. Nadia Comaneci contributed an essay about her father.

Garner, Joe. *And the Crowd Goes Wild.* Naperville, IL: Sourcebooks, Inc., 1999.

Grumeza, Ion. *Nadia: The Success Secrets of the Amazing Romanian Gymnast.* New York: K. S. Giniger Co., 1977.

Gutman, Bill. *Modern Women Superstars.* New York: Dodd, Mead and Company, 1977.

Haney, Lynn. *Perfect Balance: The Story of an Elite Gymnast.* New York: G.P. Putnam's Sons, 1979.

Harrison, Barbara Grizzuti. *The Astonishing World.* New York: Ticknor and Fields, 1992. This book contains the essay "Nadia Comaneci," which originally appeared in *Life.*

Karolyi, Bela, and Nancy Ann Richardson. *Feel No Fear: The Power, Passion, and Politics of a Life in Gymnastics.* New York: Hyperion, 1994.

Lessa, Christina. *Gymnastics Balancing Acts.* New York: Universe Publishing, 1997.

Lessa, Christina. *Women Who Win: Stories of Triumph in Sport and in Life.* New York: Universe Publishing, 1998.

Miklowitz, Gloria D. *Nadia Comaneci*. New York: Grosset and Dunlap, 1977.

Retton, Mary Lou, and Bela Karolyi. *Mary Lou: Creating an Olympic Champion*. With John Powers. New York: McGraw-Hill Book Company, 1986.

Sullivan, George. *Great Lives: Sports*. New York: Charles Scribner's Sons, 1988.

Tsui, Cristy. *Women's Gymnastics Trivia*. Chicago, IL: Handstand Media, Inc., 2001.

Welden, Amelie. *Girls Who Rocked the World*. Milwaukee, WI: Gareth Stevens Publishing, 1999.

Wimmer, Dick, editor. *The Women's Game*. Short Hills, NJ: Burford Books, Inc., 2000.

Zannos, Susan. *Female Stars of Nutrition and Weight Control*. Bear, DE: Mitchell Lane Publishers, Inc., 2001.

Appendix C: About the Author

It was a dark and stormy night. Suddenly a cry rang out, and on a hot summer night in 1954, Josephine, wife of Carl Bruce, gave birth to a boy—me. Unfortunately, this young married couple allowed Reuben Saturday, Josephine's brother, to name their first-born. Reuben, aka "The Joker," decided that Bruce was a nice name, so he decided to name me Bruce Bruce. I have gone by my middle name—David—ever since.

Being named Bruce David Bruce hasn't been all bad. Bank tellers remember me very quickly, so I don't often have to show an ID. It can be fun in charades, also. When I was a counselor as a teenager at Camp Echoing Hills in Warsaw, Ohio, a fellow counselor gave the signs for "sounds like" and "two words," then she pointed to a bruise on her leg twice. Bruise Bruise? Oh yeah, Bruce Bruce is the answer!

Uncle Reuben, by the way, gave me a haircut when I was in kindergarten. He cut my hair short and shaved a small bald spot on the back of my head. My mother wouldn't let me go to school until the bald spot grew out again.

Of all my brothers and sisters (six in all), I am the only transplant to Athens, Ohio. I was born in Newark, Ohio, and have lived all around Southeastern Ohio. However, I moved to Athens to go to Ohio University and have never left.

At Ohio U, I never could make up my mind whether to major in English or Philosophy, so I got a bachelor's degree with a double major in both areas, then I added a Master of Arts degree in English and a Master of Arts degree in Philosophy. Yes, I have my MAMA degree.

Currently, and for a long time to come (I eat fruits and veggies), I am spending my retirement writing books such as *Nadia Comaneci: Perfect 10*, *The Funniest People in Dance*, *Homer's* Iliad: *A Retelling in Prose*, and *William Shakespeare's* Othello: *A Retelling in Prose.*

Appendix D: Some Books by David Bruce

Children's Biography

Nadia Comaneci: Perfect Ten

Collections of Anecdotes

250 Anecdotes About Religion

250 Anecdotes About Religion: Volume 2

Be a Work of Art: 250 Anecdotes and Stories

The Coolest People in Art: 250 Anecdotes

The Coolest People in the Arts: 250 Anecdotes

The Coolest People in Books: 250 Anecdotes

The Coolest People in Comedy: 250 Anecdotes

Create, Then Take a Break: 250 Anecdotes

Don't Fear the Reaper: 250 Anecdotes

The Funniest People in Art: 250 Anecdotes

The Funniest People in Books: 250 Anecdotes

The Funniest People in Books, Volume 2: 250 Anecdotes

The Funniest People in Books, Volume 3: 250 Anecdotes

The Funniest People in Comedy: 250 Anecdotes

The Funniest People in Dance: 250 Anecdotes

The Funniest People in Families: 250 Anecdotes

The Funniest People in Families, Volume 2: 250 Anecdotes

The Funniest People in Families, Volume 3: 250 Anecdotes

The Funniest People in Families, Volume 4: 250 Anecdotes

The Funniest People in Families, Volume 5: 250 Anecdotes

The Funniest People in Families, Volume 6: 250 Anecdotes

The Funniest People in Movies: 250 Anecdotes

The Funniest People in Music: 250 Anecdotes

The Funniest People in Music, Volume 2: 250 Anecdotes

The Funniest People in Music, Volume 3: 250 Anecdotes

The Funniest People in Neighborhoods: 250 Anecdotes

The Funniest People in Relationships: 250 Anecdotes

The Funniest People in Sports: 250 Anecdotes

The Funniest People in Sports, Volume 2: 250 Anecdotes

The Funniest People in Television and Radio: 250 Anecdotes

The Funniest People in Theater: 250 Anecdotes

The Funniest People Who Live Life: 250 Anecdotes

The Funniest People Who Live Life, Volume 2: 250 Anecdotes

The Kindest People Who Do Good Deeds, Volume 1: 250 Anecdotes

The Kindest People Who Do Good Deeds, Volume 2: 250 Anecdotes

Maximum Cool: 250 Anecdotes

The Most Interesting People in Movies: 250 Anecdotes

The Most Interesting People in Politics and History: 250 Anecdotes

The Most Interesting People in Politics and History, Volume 2: 250 Anecdotes

The Most Interesting People in Politics and History, Volume 3: 250 Anecdotes

The Most Interesting People in Religion: 250 Anecdotes

The Most Interesting People in Sports: 250 Anecdotes

The Most Interesting People Who Live Life: 250 Anecdotes

The Most Interesting People Who Live Life, Volume 2: 250 Anecdotes

Reality is Fabulous: 250 Anecdotes and Stories

Resist Psychic Death: 250 Anecdotes

Seize the Day: 250 Anecdotes and Stories

Retellings of a Classic Work of Literature

Dante's Divine Comedy: *A Retelling in Prose*

The Trojan War and Its Aftermath: Four Ancient Epic Poems

William Shakespeare's 38 Plays: Retellings in Prose